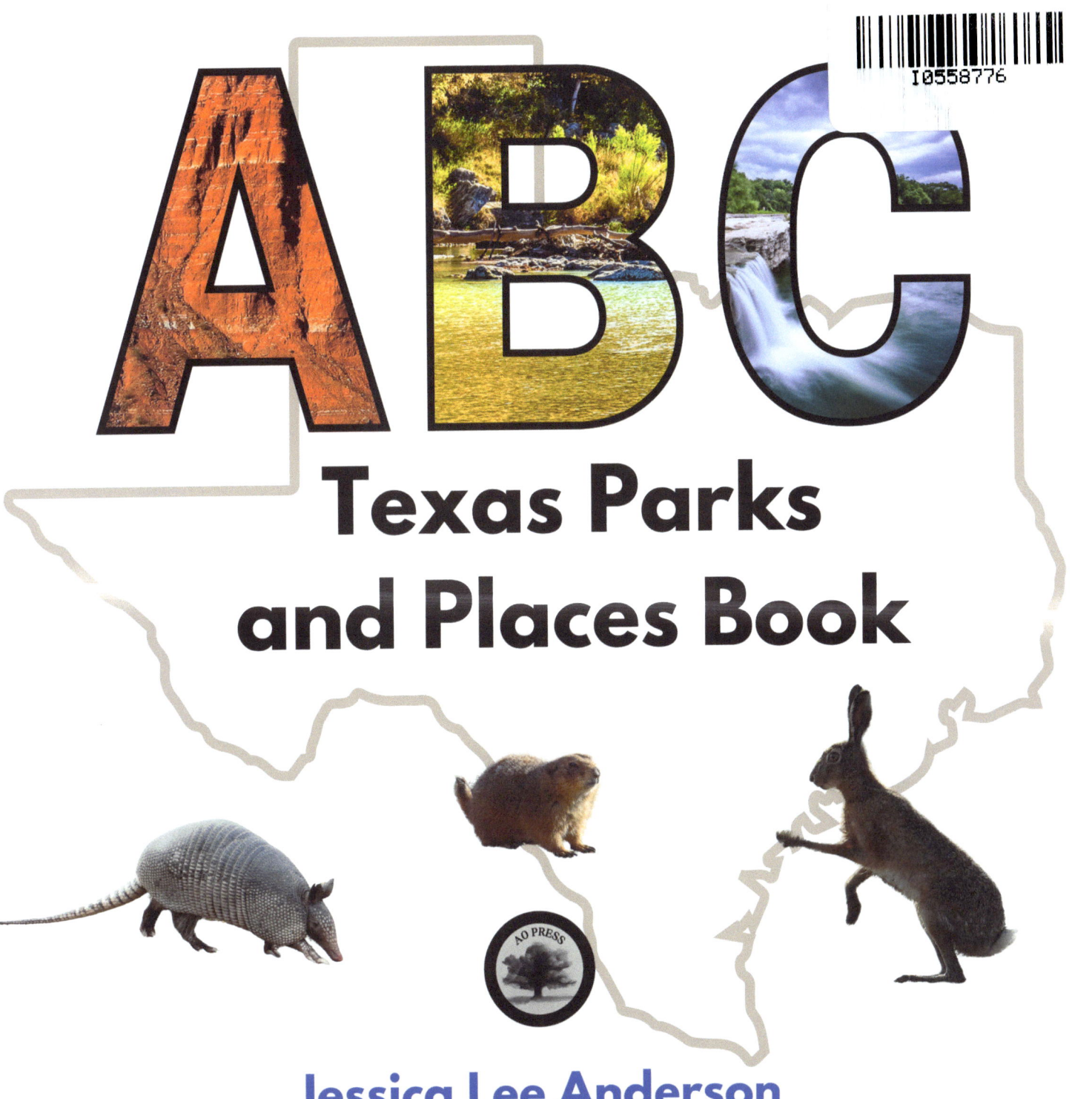

ABC

Texas Parks and Places Book

Jessica Lee Anderson

Paperback ISBN: 979-8-9899560-8-1

To everyone who helps conserve the diverse beauty and history of Texas - JLA

Photo credits—Front cover: Jeffrey D. Smoot (Palo Duro Canyon State Park), Richard McMillin (Guadalupe River State Park), keeweeboy (McKinney Falls State Park), Harry Collins (coyote), Maxfocus (mule deer), Jim Johnsen (javelina); Back cover: Ariel Casas (Palo Duro Canyon State Park); Cover page: Jeffrey D. Smoot (Palo Duro Canyon State Park), Richard McMillin (Guadalupe River State Park), keeweeboy (McKinney Falls State Park), Lisay (armadillo), munro1 (black-tailed prairie dog), predrag1 (blakctailed jackrabbit); Copyright page: jzabloski (roadrunner), cturtletrax (eastern hognose), Dedication page: Leong Kok Weng (Brazos Bend State Park), p. 4: Karolina Images, Traveler1116; p. 5: Wirestock, Peter Blottman Photography; p. 6: Lena Oldums, Jupiter Images, p. 7: Jessica Lee Anderson; p. 8: Clendenen, Roschetzkylstockphoto; p. 9: Michael Anderson; p. 10: Richard McMillin; p. 11: milehightraveler, EntropyWorskhop; p. 12: Natalia Silyanov, Jennifer Coulter; p. 13: Kanokwalee Pusitanun, Artby Allyson; p. 14: milehightraveler, John Fox; p. 15: Richard McMillin, p. 16: Jessica Lee Anderson.; p. 17: zrfphoto, Denis Tangney Jr.; p. 18: Nathan Wasylewski, Jessica Lee Anderson; p. 19: Darren E. Tromblay, Cracker Clips Stock Media; p. 20: Ronda Kimbrow, Michael Anderson; p. 21: Trong Nguyen; p. 22: milehightraveler, artiste9999; p. 23: Wirestock; p. 24: JLFCapture. Tim Speer; p. 25: Katie Dobies, milehightraveler; p. 26: OneKnight, Ernest Esquivel; p. 27: ferrantraite, Ken Hartlein; p. 28: Michael Anderson, p. 29: LaVonna Moore, Lisay; p. 30: DAPA Images, Life on White; p. 31: Michael Anderson

This Book Belongs to:

_____

 is for Alamo Historic Site

The Alamo is a historic Spanish mission in San Antonio with a fascinating history. This was the site of the Battle of the Alamo during the Texas Revolution.

A a

B is for Big Bend Ranch State Park

Big Bend Ranch State Park (near Big Bend National Park) is the largest state park in Texas! The park spans over 300,000 acres and includes mountains, canyons, desert areas, and dark skies perfect for stargazing.

C is for Caprock Canyon State Park

Caprock Canyon State Park is in the Texas Panhandle, a place carved by wind, water, and time. The park shelters wildlife and also the Texas State Bison Herd.

C c

is for Davis Mountains State Park

Davis Mountains State Park, located in Fort Davis (West Texas), offers many outdoor adventures. People have hunted and camped here for thousands of years, long before this place became a state park during the Great Depression.

D d

E is for Enchanted Rock State Natural Area

Enchanted Rock State Natural Area features an ancient pink granite dome and many other fascinating rock features. The park is full of legends and myths, especially as the granite creaks and groans when it warms from the sun and cools at night.

E e

F is for Fort Richardson State Park and Historic Site

You can find Fort Richardson State Park and Historic Site in Jacksboro, northwest of Fort Worth. Several buildings still stand at what used to be a large U.S. Army installation.

F f

 is for Garner State Park

You can discover Garner State Park in the Texas Hill Country. The park features high mesas and deep canyons, and the scenic Frio River reflects bald cypress trees that line the banks.

G g

is for Hueco Tanks State Park and Historic Site

Hueco Tanks State Park and Historic Site is located in El Paso. In ancient times, visitors came to the rock hills in search of <u>huecos</u> (rainwater pooled in natural rock basins), and some of these people created images on the rocks.

 is for Inks Lake State Park

Inks Lake State Park is northwest of Austin in the Hill Country city of Burnet. The park is a place to enjoy water activities (even cliff jumping), hiking, and viewing nature including wildflowers.

Ii

J is for Jamaica Beach

Jamaica Beach is a public beach area on Galveston Island next to Galveston Island State Park. Galveston Island State Park has a nature center you can explore, and the park features both bay and beach attractions along with miles of trails, camp sites, and more.

Jj

 is for Kickapoo Cavern State Park

Kickapoo Cavern State Park (west of San Antonio in Brackettville) features caves that are home to Mexican free-tailed bats and other animals like skunks, coyotes, porcupines, bees, snakes, and even the occasional black bear or two. Guided cave tours are available by reservation.

L is for Lost Maples State Natural Area

Along the Sabinal River, Lost Maples State Natural Area is best known for its spectacular fall colors. The park is located in Vanderpool (northwest of San Antonio), and you can birdwatch, hike a tall cliff, stargaze, and much more.

M is for Monahans Sandhills State Park

![Sand dune field at sunset]

Monahans Sandhills State Park is in West Texas near Odessa. Here you can climb a sand dune field —an "ocean of sand" that the wind whips around to form peaks and valleys that change constantly.

M m

 is for National Parks

Texas is home to two national parks—Big Bend and Guadalupe Mountains (pictured). Texas also has several recreation areas, national monuments, preserves, historic sites, and a seashore that all fall under the protection of the National Park Service.

O is for Old Tunnel State Park

Old Tunnel State Park (in Fredericksburg) is the smallest state park in Texas! The park is named after a railroad tunnel cut through a limestone hill, now home to millions of Mexican free-tailed bats and thousands of cave myotis bats.

P is for Pedernales Falls State Park

![Pedernales Falls State Park photograph]

Pedernales Falls State Park, west of Austin, is named after the Pedernales River. Water flows over slabs of ancient limestone—it can rise quickly in a flash flood!

Pp

Q is for Quintana Beach

Quintana Beach has many sandy acres of beach along the Texas Gulf Coast. The Justin Hurst Wildlife Management Area is nearby along with the Quintana Neotropical Bird Sanctuary.

Qq

R is for Ray Roberts Lake State Park

Ray Roberts Lake State Park is one of the most visited state parks in Texas! The park is an hour north of the Dallas/Fort Worth area, and there are nine units with many opportunities for you to play in the water and explore on land.

R r

S is for Seminole Canyon State Park and Historic Site

![Seminole Canyon landscape]

Seminole Canyon State Park is located along the Rio Grande River near the city of Del Rio. Ancient people dwelled in the canyon here, and thousands of years ago, people painted pictographs in the rock shelters.

T is for Tyler State Park

Tyler State Park is in Tyler, nestled in the Pineywoods of Northeast Texas. The park has a lake for you to enjoy, woodland areas to investigate, and lots of wildlife viewing opportunities.

Tt

 is for Uncertain, Texas

Uncertain, Texas is a town in East Texas near Caddo Lake State Park and the Caddo Lake National Wildlife Refuge. The lake was named for the Caddoan people who once called this area home, and the lake harbors many species of fish as well as alligators.

V is for Village Creek State Park

Village Creek State Park lies on the edge of the Big Thicket National Preserve in East Texas, close to Beaumont. Village Creek is one of the few free-flowing creeks in Texas, and some alligators live in the park.

 is for Wyler Aerial Tramway

While the future of Wyler Aerial Tramway is unknown because of safety concerns, it was once an exciting way to take in views of the Franklin Mountains (pictured). You can hike, rock climb, bike, camp, and more at Franklin Mountains State Park.

Ww

 **is for XIT**

The XIT Ranch once spanned over three million acres in the Panhandle (photo of the abandoned headquarters), and the XIT Museum in Dalhart has a mission to preserve this history. The annual XIT Rodeo and Reunion is known for being the "World's Largest Free Barbecue."

X x

Y is for Yegua Creek Park

Yegua Creek Park is located at Lake Somerville near Lake Somerville State Park and Trailway (pictured). Both of these parks offer opportunities to fish, boat, paddle, swim, hike, and more.

Yy

Z is for Zaragoza Birthplace State Historic Site

Zaragoza Birthplace State Historic Site is located near Presidio La Bahia (a fort built by the Spanish Army). General Zaragoza led the Mexican Army to independence from France on May 5, 1862—this is celebrated every year at Cinco de Mayo.

5 Texas State Park Facts:

 A state agency called Texas Parks & Wildlife Department manages and protects the wildlife in Texas along with their habitats.

 Texas State Parks have a mission to protect "Texas' vast natural and cultural beauty" (since 1923).

 Mother Neff State Park (in Waco) was the first state park in Texas! Isabella Neff donated land in 1921, and the State Parks Board became official in 1923.

 The CCC, or Civilian Conservation Corps (a group enlisted in work programs during the Great Depression), built many parks in Texas.

 Visit https://tpwd.texas.gov to learn more about parks in Texas and to make plans and reservations.

Jessica Lee Anderson is an award-winning author of over 75 books for young readers. Jessica lives near Austin, Texas with her daughter, Ava, and husband, Michael. They have a passion for camping and exploring parks. You can learn more about Jessica by visiting **www.jessicaleeanderson.com.**

Check out these other titles:

www.ingramcontent.com/pod-product-compliance
Lightning Source LLC
Chambersburg PA
CBHW041501120626
46547CB00003B/495